Tandem

The Rengay Journal

Tandem: The Rengay Journal
Volume 2, Number 1

ISBN: 978-1-7779767-2-9

https://www.tandem-the-rengay-journal.net

Cover Art: Jim Force (aka Nika)
Photo Manipulation: Ignatius Fay

Tandem

Noun: a group of two people or machines working together;

Adverb: alongside each other; together.

Adjective: having two things arranged one in front of the other; one behind the other.

Rengay — A Growth Genre

Rengay continues to grow in popularity, and particularly quickly in the last two years. That may seem counterintuitive at first glance because of the pervasive restrictions on personal movement and interaction that have dominated our lives in that time. The key, I think, is the multitude of interactive media, such as Zoom and FaceTime, that enjoy such wide-spread usage now. Many people who, not long ago, had never used nor even heard of some of these utilities are now using them regularly.

These online communication tools explain another interesting trend. Not only do they allow poets to collaborate, albeit not truly 'face-to-face,' but they make it easy for people all over the world to work together. I am seeing a rise in submissions from collaborators who live in widely separate parts of the world. For example, someone living in India would have much difficulty writing with someone in the US if they had to use snail mail or email. And the cost of meeting in person is usually prohibitive.

Whatever the reason, we welcome this growth trend and hope that it continues. That being said, the desire to get together, to meet in person, is an insistent itch that we hope to be able to scratch in the near future.

From the Editors

Raise your hand if you are beginning to show symptoms of cabin fever, of being cut-off from people and places who are important to you. I know several poets who are feeling unmotivated and attribute the lack to the fact that haiku have their source in experience. So many people have not been anywhere outside the necessary for so long that they are starving for inspiration. The negative effects of this isolation have been much more debilitating for these poets than Covid-19 itself. On the other hand, some report having more time to sit in their gardens, to watch the flowers grow and the activities of creatures great and small.

From a collaborative point of view, we are lucky to have Zoom. We can still meet to share experiences and to write together. The editorial staff hope that the contents of this issue will provide a small beacon to illuminate your poetic souls and provide a bit of respite.

We have decided to make a tradition of including a poem containing *tandem* on page 7. At first, the idea seemed unfeasible because we knew of only a couple of *tandem* poems. Charles Trumbull graceously agreed to cull his massive database of haiku for such poems, and we were right—not many. Charles located only twenty, but at two issues per year, we should be good for ten years. Thanks so much, Charles. Greatly appreciated.

Unfortunately, Seren Fargo's ability to contribute to the editing of this issue was seriously reduced due to tribulations on a personal level. She suggested that we approach Angela Terry who generously agreed to step in as guest editor. We are grateful for her capable assistance this time round.

Finally, congratulations to Jacquie Pearce and Alan S. Bridges for their wonderful poem, *It's &^%$#@* Hot!*, which is the Editors' Choice as Best of *Tandem* v. 1, no. 2. See it on the outside back cover.

Once again, we we are gratified that so many poets contributed good poems for this issue! We appreciate your support, from all over the world.

no passing zone
two yellow leaves tumble
in tandem

Joann Klontz
Raw NerVZ 6:3 (Fall 1999)

Contents

Stardust

ancient pond—
sounds of life
I cannot see

gathering dusk
one splash then another

the crackle
of the arc lighter...
mouthwatering

moonrise
a soloist jump-starts
the chorus

paddling alone
with the Milky Way

stardust
the stones
I never skipped

Ryland Shengzhi Li
Cynthia Anderson

Where The Lighthouse Was

by wind and waves
chiseled in place
sea stacks

a volleyball shard
my misspent dotage

cliffside road
closed half a century ago
yellow lupin

ocean sun
the silhouette of a hawk
missing a tail feather

fishermen with their families
mending nets on the beach

new moon
the sound of surf crashing
where the lighthouse was

John Thompson
Chuck Brickley

Sky Songs

giving way to the sun
how the mist swarms
the placid lake before

a blue heron
slowly descends to earth

mountain meadow
revealed in the mist
a dream

blue over blue
skies and seas
a gull spreads its wings

once before moonrise
these twilight moments...

followed the moon
from east to west
and it's dawn

Ram Chandran
Nithya

Life Like A River

a river
braids through salt marsh
streaks of dawn

the kicked stone
wakes a marsh wren

lone sora calling
hidden in pickleweed
cattails sway in a breeze

high noon
a slow stalking bittern
shimmers in heat waves

a pair of snow geese
flap up in tandem

evening fog settles
the river trickles
to the sea

Marcyn Del Clements

Floral

a school
of sunflowers
turns my head

daffodils
my footsteps lighten

I pretend
you walk next to me
holding my bouquet

scent of lilacs
the reblooming
of memories

gazing into wisteria
my eyes fill with purple tears

falling
into my shadow
blossoms

Genie Nakano
Jackie Chou

Ikebana

garden shrine
the balance of branches
in an earthen bowl

stumbling about in lilacs
a bumble bee

milkweed silk
an old monk walks
in the wind

placed just so
between heaven and earth
a morning glory

still life of a sunflower
offering seeds

ikebana
how a twig bends
the heart

Anton R. Kelian
Sue Colpitts

At Last Light

heat lightning
the air's pinkish tinge
at dusk

out in the marsh
one last sweep for supper

among the reeds
leopard frogs serenade—
the setting sun

last light
the nasal "peent" of nighthawks
announces spring

first stars—
a barn owl swivels its head

a field mouse
slips home to her pups
safe—for now

Ignatius Fay
Marcyn Del Clements

Looking Out

lockdown
a doe with her twins
at the playground

gathering dust
the thermos for hot soup

window view
in the woodpecker's beak
a red berry

at last a path
through the fallen leaves
food delivery

a new addition
celebrated on Zoom

my careless hair
and pale face dare come out
moon in the clouds

Marilyn Ashbaugh
Jeanne Cook

Chores

worn so many places
the new detergent
burns her hands

car wash
the door grabs her flare skirt

wiping away sweat
stubborn grease
stuck to the pot

evening breeze
the tantalizing aroma
of fresh coffee

again the timer…
beeps on the microwave

shucking corn
a wood duck waddles
closer

M. R. Defibaugh
Christina Chin

Faded Love

easily bruised pears ...
to think we once loved
unconditionally

where we carved our names
woodpecker holes

orange poppies
able to weather any storm
yet wilting at my touch

Ouija board
the magic of her smile
in an old photo

our argument interrupted
by a perfect rainbow

an old record
its pops and hisses
remembered kiss

John Thompson
Garry Gay

Golden State

slipping
into the pool at midnight
hot embers

another cherry-red sunset
high winds whip the flames

after the wildfires
a great horned owl's
golden stare

moonlight filters
through singed live oak
first scent of rain

through thick ash
a superbloom

back-country hike
matilija poppies glow
in the twilight

Dyana Basist
Billie Dee

Shoreline

jagged rockfall
below a limestone cliff
the smell of wet rock

looking for fossils
under a slab, a coiled snake

the scent of spruce—
steep ascent
turns hikers back

gnarled cliff-top pines
bent away from the ocean
doe and fawn

climbing a hop hornbeam
black bear cubs

rodent tooth marks
in the pumpernickel
fish on the campfire

Janice Doppler
Ignatius Fay

Gaia

the ocean floor
changes position
starry flounder

the insatiate shiver
of the nestling's wings

friend or foe?
one ant taps another
with its antennae

housebound humans
the pulse of the earth
softens

a doe raises her head
to meet my gaze

nightly ritual
watching my prayer plant
fold its leaves

Sheila Sondik
Seren Fargo

Ripples of Disharmony

crude oil seep
the heart rate
of a blue fin tuna

a young boy
reels in a sunken can

bycatch
of a fishing net
whale song

bobbing in rhythm
empty bottles
enmeshed in lines

albatross bird count
body count

pumping away
offshore rigs
and rainbows

Deborah P Kolodji
Richard L. Matta

Overboard

fluttering
the sails of a maxi
near the finish

live crayfish on display
at the floating fish shop

cold beers
the winning skipper
tossed overboard

crimson sunset
the Regatta Queen
adds more lipstick

the scent of sunscreen
mingles with hot chips

signal flags
flutter in and out
of the moon

Lorraine Haig
Ron C. Moss

In the Ebb and Flow

the dog and I
followed by the waves
not a trace

a row of pink shells
on her windowsill

letting the moon
slowly tug
before I answer

mangrove crabs
the click and suck
at low tide

oar rhythms in our arms
after the narrows

manoeuvring
among the jellyfish
deep-water swell

Kristen Lang
Lorraine Haig

On the Rocks

twinkle of muscovite
halfway through
a second martini

slurring, she calls him
a mica schist

all this talk
of cleavage...
his Old Fashioned, sweating

back from the loo
the conversation turns
to coprolites

shaken, not stirred
his flinty glare

third nightcap
the rise and fall
in a lava lamp

Tanya McDonald
Lew Watts

Full Disclosure

island breeze
the scent of lilacs
through an open window

mom's jewelry box opened
to sneak a necklace

third birthday…
the largest gift
opened first

my heart opens
to the prairie sky

white sand beach
the open shell
I step over

alone in a nest
the open-mouthed chick

Susan Constable
Wilda Morris
Michael Dylan Welch

Cutting Loose

together
in this cosmic bubble
solar winds

auroras on each planet
stretched magnetospheres

distant family
the 10,000 year orbit
of Sedna

Lowell Observatory
we hold a requiem
for Pluto

termination shock
divorce settlement

Voyager I
breaks through the heliosphere...
trying to call home

Deborah P Kolodji
Billie Dee

Discontinuity

snow falling
behind my eyelids
imaginary numbers

in the fractal blizzard
all flakes vibrate in unison

bare branches
everything the algorithm
misses

aspen grove
a matrix of messages
pulses through the sap

power outage
finding x by candlelight

human caused
lightning ignites the forest
an unbalanced equation

Lisa Gerlits
j rap

midnight moon

bullfrog and Buddha
contemplating
the garden's beauty

a bee hip-deep
in a daisy

cold wind…
curled in the dog house
our cat and kittens

again the dog
sleeps on the porch

chicken coop
only the fox
still awake

fireflies circle
the midnight moon

Nika
Margaret Rutley
Sidney Bending

Left Behind

frosted window
the moth still
hanging on

last leaf
the letter she left

dove song
her suicide journal
one page long

empty moon
visiting all the places
she used to be

the dark matter
of memories

hard rain
the softness
of her pillow

Bryan Rickert
Kat Lehman

Tethered

returning home
the sweetness
of Bing cherries

at the birdhouse door
fledgling sparrows

through slats in the fence
a conversation
with the neighbor

dangling
from the old swing set
Concord grapes

tethered to his garden
sunflowers

from yard to yard
the meandering path
of a calico cat

Alan S. Bridges
Jacquie Pearce

Street Teens

jeans
that made her ass look big
Christmas charity

too heavy to carry in
home gym mirrors

good will donation—
at the soup kitchen
someone wears my shirt

as much as clothes
can say about a man
Coke is it!

homeless
threadbare coat clutched to her throat

parked
across from the food bank
ice cream truck

Ignatius Fay
Rob Piotrowski

Wasting Time

the children laugh
about my childhood
raisin days

an old box of toys
found in the attic

squeaky metronome
the hours on a swing set
across the street

long summer days
fried bologna cut
into strips

friends scatter
with the streetlights

lost in tall weeds
the wiffle ball
the memories

Kat Lehmann
Bryan Rickert

High n' Dry

crowded bar
I don't know what
I want here

a swizzle stick
with nothing to swizzle

the bartender
brings a martini
stirred, not shaken

ladies dancing
scent of cold vodka

corner booth
a flickering candle
next to the tip

last call…
home alone again

Agnes Eva Savich
Terri L. French
Raymond A. French

A Deep Groove

all their lights
on a timer
winter sun

meals on wheels
while the meatloaf is warm

deer trail
a deep groove worn
into the saltlick

sideways
what the bark holds
for the nuthatch

trees strung
with hawthorn berries

this month's check
their footsteps
down the snowy lane

Julie Schwerin
Dan Schwerin

Mermaid's Tears

a lonely child
with her plastic pail…
collecting mermaid's tears

sand dollars
stranded by the tide

holding the secrets
of the sea
conch shell (at her feet)

under new ownership
a hermit crab
moves in

almost as if
the barnacles could talk

for a time
the world becomes smaller
tide pool

Angela Terry
Julie Schwerin

In the Park Wind

tautened robe
a child blows down
the statue's leg

dust clouds
hide his face

lost sandals
in the fountain
her sunburnt feet

rippling
in the shallow water
small shadows

a beggar counts
what's left

gathering dusk
the distant coo
of pigeons

Richard Thomas
Hifsa Ashraf

Then and Now

sidewalk chalk
my children drew
their hearts out

diy face masks the old fabric of our lives

that new normal
at 6 pm her street broke
into song

sporting a shaggy cut his own hair

we made do
with a splash of juice
our quarantini

social distancing still I ask myself for a hug

Laszlo Slomovits
Michele Root-Bernstein
Jennifer Burd

Flowers and the Human Condition

busy thoroughfare
veil of white wisteria
covers the old porch

murmuring passers-by...
blue poppies

the crunch of gravel—
buttercups
line the path

blackberries in bloom
a bulldozer wrestles
the tree stump

remembering your death...
the Rose of Sharon blossoms

wedding chapel
every bouquet
has baby's breath

Kathleen Tice
Richard Tice

Unlikely Blooms

office ikebana
a plethora
of blossoms

folding my fate
origami roses

I pick
a cactus flower
for my hair

scent of sunshine
the century plant's
glorious life

sprouting from sandy soil
seven blue pups

downy tufts
of dandelions
blown away

kris moon kondo
Jackie Chou
Kath Abela Wilson
Sigrid Saradunn
Diane Funston
genie nakano

Hair

autumn wind
the oak tree's
fiery red afro

the tallest of beehives
sings 'be my baby'

Angela Davis
pulls back her hair
the great escape

recapturing
the braids mother made
for my gypsy look

flowing curls peek
from the babushka

I try
a Medusa look
locks of snakes

Jackie Chou
kris moon kondo
genie nakano
Kath Abela Wilson
Sigrid Saradunn
Diane Funston

Salty Memories

sea foam
on your lips
my cappuccino

slathered on his chin
her aromatic fish sauce

he imagines her
on the half shell
oyster liquor

body shot
tasting her navel
in the screwdriver

tears begin and end
with a kiss

salty memories
two olive in the bottom
of a martini glass

Joshua St. Claire
Amber Winter

Words, Words, Words

closed bookshop
Shakespeare's neon quill
scribbling away

each whirling swirl
part of the river's dissertation

southern breeze
... strange fruit hanging
from the poplar trees

drifting together
for a while and then apart
skywritten hearts

journal ashes in the fireplace
spark one last word

inner city—
the subway graffiti
silently howl

Chuck Brickley
John Thompson

Out & Back Again

swimsuit pockets
full of skipping stones
I couldn't let go of

throwing away
my fat sweaters

bad fit
to have and to keep
the engagement ring

returning
to my childhood
the boomerang

my didgeridoo
circular breathing-challenged

sunrise
a joey jumps
out of his pouch

John Thompson
Margie Gustafson
Jackie Maugh Robinson
Lew Watts
Marcyn Del Clements
Jayashree Maniyil

Bitter News

morning coffee
gives me a boost
these up and down days

bitter news sugar coated
by caramel swirls

swerve
a natural sweetener
still tastes fake

whipped cream topping
his white lies
covered up

milk in the refrigerator
spoils within ten days

brief romance
the heart-shaped foam
melting

Genie Nakano
Jackie Chou

Through Tree Leaves

rising sun
aslant rays coruscate
the forest mist

from rococo clouds
God-light spills outside the frame

silhouettes
caught contre-jour
leaf shadows' dance

fern brushed path
edged in tones of green
frond symmetry

dappled footprints morph
a chameleon freezes

last shimmering
the flight of light
on crow wing

Anton R. Kelian
Sue Colpitts

ESL

hanging out the clothes
she hears the parrots call
the wind is changing

mom and her budgie
talking to each other

donated greys
cussing in different accents
zoo closed to re-train

parakeet
at the shiny steel kettle
a new bird

Halloween Party
I go as my green conure

Indian ringneck
with clipped flight feathers
more blue language

Marcyn Del Clements
Ignatius Fay

Life's Moments

fledgling romance
all the battles won
without a fight

lovers' lane
lovegrass on their jeans

drawn gently towards
its red centre
desert rose

friar's snowdrops
by the sanctuary church
sanctus bells

stage 4
anniversary dance

crocuses break
through the winter gloom
season's change

M. R. Defibaugh
Christina Chin

Flower'tudes

starting in the foothills
the poppies steadily work
up the mountainsides

window box
already sprouting dandelions

none of the buds
seem to want to go first—
morning glory

seed pack
in the back of the drawer
late spring

in the dusky glow a trumpet vine
filled with the buzzing of bees

wild primrose
somewhere under it
her mailbox

John Thompson
Garry Gay

Sonoma

between the sets
of reds and whites
tasting crackers

view of the vineyard
pinot grigio

taste of tannin
a spiral staircase
to the wine cellar

oak barrels
nutmeg in the zinfandel
tasting notes

scent of blueberry
in the swirling syrah

dark chocolate
we finish our flight
with port

Richard L. Matta
Deborah P Kolodji

Green Gleam

lemon light
waking to the liquid notes
of the butcherbird

a pink robin hops over
the nest of snowflakes

crowded city mall
a white ibis stops
to preen

even in all
that endless blue sky…
a superb fairy wren

a green gleam
on the teal's head

deeper still
the yellow eye
of a currawong

Lorraine Haig
Ron C. Moss

Breathless

first bird note
the air above the lake
polished silver

foggy tendrils
tangled in the trees

a dragonfly
too cold to move
slow-curving reed

pale sunlight
a mountain range
shapes the horizon

faint-peppered gold
in a murmur of ripples

water's edge
a wallaby
nibbling moss

Kristen Lang
Lorraine Haig

Mocking The Lyre

autumn chill
after the skinny dip
tawny owls

olive-sided flycatcher
spooked by a belch

dew dripping
from the cattails
American bittern

California quail
the hitchhiker's sign
says Chicago

who's a pretty boy, then
lost budgie

hot pants
at the bus stop
a lone starling

Lew Watts
Tanya McDonald

Illumination

pink and purple afterglow
lovers stroll on the beach
distant lightning

whittling by the campfire
crackling curls of basswood

she drops
his harmonica in the sand
he kicks a stump

a rumble of thunder
he pours wine on the flames
hiss of hot embers

crawling into sleeping bags
lantern-lit tent

side by side in silence
he reaches for her hand
flicker of fireflies

Wilda Morris
Jo Balistreri

Toxic

warning rattle
from a coiled snake
fresh gossip

taking her night pills
foxgloves outside the window

black widow spider
nobody wants to wear
a mask

potatoes sprouting
in the pantry
rubber bullets

poison oak
your rash tweets

unsent letter
I switch from vitriol
to blue ink

Deborah P Kolodji
Billie Dee

Trailing Off

cold rain
blown in on the wind
a cicada's wing

thunder dusk
the path flickers

hiking out
our doubling
strides

sudden squall
a shelter of packs
and pine

the rising
needle scent

dry indoors
the yearn
to return

Bryan Rickert
Kat Lehmann

Diminuendo

daybreak
the bugle
of a sandhill crane

from a rooftop
a flicker's rat-a-tat-tat

after the rain
the inside-out call
of a willie wagtail

down bare branches
a cascade
of chickadee-dees

through my cellphone
the buzz of a rubythroat's wings

nightfall
the crow stops cawing
for her missing mate

Alan S. Bridges
Jacquie Pearce

Spinster's Garden

frost warning
a one winged moth
beats a circle

pumpkins rotting
on the vine

morning silence
cicadas and their shells
side by side

spinster's garden
the whirligig
out of control

empty tomato plants
hang from their cage

full corn moon
a golden glimmer
on black ice

Bryan Rickert
Terri L. French

What the Gargoyle Witnessed

petrichor
earthworms bubble up
between daisies

compost layers unfold
graveyard shadows

lurking
in the cathedral
birdsong

abandoned binky
surrounded by ripples
stratocumulus

burgundy lace
across her catafalque

crossroads' echo
blood squirms beneath
my retina

Joshua Gage
Agnes Eva Savich

An unconventional Exquisite Corpse rengay, written every other word instead of verse. Authorship: petrichor (JG), earthworms (AES), bubble (JG), up (AES), etc.

Patch of Moonlight

newly single
the comfort
of minor league games

the long wait for a table
for one

what she wears
in place of a wedding band
berry moon

stargazing...
the company
of fireflies

a patch of moonlight
on the morning glory and trellis

on a whim
a little water
for the bleeding heart

Dan Schwerin
Julie Schwerin

Finally Falling

mid October
a full-bloom iris
in its own season

too long after
his aftershave

hothouse tomatoes
a new year's resolution
to go raw

let the teens mock
our winter day in bed

finally falling
for spring rain
oak leaves

carousel ride
grandma grabs the brass ring

Laszlo Slomovits
Michele Root-Bernstein
Jennifer Burd

Washboard Lane

where the backbone
connects to the hip bone
washboard lane

this year's "name your favorite
pothole" contest

wager among friends—
turns out I can't
still do a cartwheel

they say you never forget
how to ride a bike—
I beg to differ

in my spring garden
a face plant

slipping
on the black ice
off the roof

Julie Schwerin
Angela Terry

Suburbia

old home driveway—
fitting my hand over
a child's handprint

row of homes leading
to the empty schoolyard

reflected in windows
the playground
and dandelion lawn

hot wind on my face
the lawn drier today

motionless night:
on TV cheery suns cover
a map of the state

rain on the roofs—
the smell of wet concrete

Jack Lyon
Richard Tice
Richard Bingham

Foxy

he brings me
inari sushi
every day

I give him back
a mischievous smile

a slinky red dress
hanging in the closet
the morning after

on the table
barefoot dancer's
come hither look

secrets hidden
under false eyelashes

long night
her playful dreams
of raw oysters

genie nakano
Kath Abela Wilson
kris moon kondo
Sigrid Saradunn
Jackie Chou
Diane Funston

Silver Linings

double duty—
for covid & wildfires
the same mask

flat tire
a meadow full of poppies

highway patrolman
tells me he's a poet too
$500 ticket

doing somersaults
on the beach
her twisted ankle

a broken cup
filled with tiny flowers

walking home
without an umbrella
distant rainbow

John Thompson
Garry Gay

Geometry

somewhere an owl
the winter triangle
high in the sky

whoosh of wings
in the square of Pegasus

full moon
reflection
Canada geese

distant calls
a mockingbird
extends Orion's belt

connecting the dots
the Big Dipper

Auriga chariot
through city haze
reminder of home

Deborah P Kolodji
Richard L. Matta

Backstreet Mozart

clear skies
a shower of coins
in the busker's hat

a tanned sinewy juggler
draws in the crowd

the crowd's ooh
a sword swallower
opens his mouth

backstreet Mozart
a violin player brings
more sunshine

around the pan piper
the space fills with children

twilight market
the blues man's slide
gives off a little spark

Lorraine Haig
Ron C. Moss

Fifty Shades

too old
for make-up
a touch of blue

page turns break the silence
a night of romance

dance class
the women partner
each other

buttercup yellow
the shelves of sensible shoes'
fifty shades of brown

halving the recipe
dinner for one

blowing dust
off the turntable—
'blame it on the blues'

Lorraine Haig
Kristen Lang

Illusions

old wooden fence
little faces
peek through knotholes

hedgerows humming
pollinators in and out

neighbors
exchanging greetings
across the picket

summer heat
the buzz of honeybees
within farmhouse walls

under the lot line
ground squirrels tunneling

song of a wood thrush
through the windbreak
we stop to listen

Wilda Morris
Jo Balistreri

Tricks of the Trade

deep winter
a raven calls
wolves to a kill

looting the squirrel's cache
a Steller's jay

gathering darkness
hundreds of crows stream
into the roost

chattering to her mate
a magpie on a branch
of elk antlers

a blue jay flies off
with a robin's egg

spring hike
a whiskey jack
unpacks our lunch

Kristen Lindquist
Jacquie Pearce

Empty Space

no life
in my life
winter walk

monochrome
sheet clouds and me

dwindling fire
this same book
as last year

returning
to your silence
journey's end

an empty space
where the cat used to be

snow drifts
the birdsong gone
unnoticed

Tia Haynes
Bryan Rickert

Wish Fulfillment

winter seclusion
falling again
for click bait

even her snail mail
full of offers she can't pass up

new windows
she didn't even know she needed
neighborhood watch

the pillows that came free
with the mattress—
redecorated guest room

the snow blower we discussed
shows up on our news feed

wish fulfillment—
the internet
plays fairy godmother

Julie Schwerin
Angela Terry

Keeping Things Fresh

flower vase
how carefully she arranges
the conversation

a cloud of baby's breath
moving his chair back

awkward silence
she trims
the ragged ends

keeping things fresh
his penny's worth

changing light
on a stem with thorns
one open bud

ikebana
those three little words

Michele Root-Bernstein
Laszlo Slomovits
Jennifer Burd

August

families sprawl
on front stoops
rumble of the El

harvesting
the last shriveled tomato

spontaneous fires
in drought-ravished hills
stores out of masks

salamander
in the dry creek
becoming a cannibal

our ginger cat stretches out
in the shade

ice cubes
in paper cups
lemonade stand

Jo Balistreri
Wilda Morris

A Day's Palette

morning song...
the low, slow turning
of the color wheel

dawn's brush
painting the sun's joy

watching the brilliance fade
from the canvas
midday melancholy

a drop of ink here and there
turning into a rainbow

palette of the day—
shared
prisms of light

shadows of dusk frame
the master's piece

Angela Terry
Cheryl Berrong
Sharon Young

Adopting and Adapting

wave-worn pebbles
the sea turtle gives herself
to the sand

bursting the balloon
spider egg sac

robin's nest
the cowbird turns her back
on the Hare Moon

abandoning hope
before their eyes
ever meet

his brood pouch
how gently she places her pearls there

adopting
and adapting
mother's love

Joshua St. Claire
Amber Winter

Bios for Editorial Board

Marcyn Del Clements, Claremont, CA, USA

Her formal/published name is Marcyn Del Clements, after a 3 century-old house in the Woodstock Woods, for the 2 sisters living there, Margorie and Cynthia, the latter, her mother. Nicknamed Marcy, after a 5,344' mountain in Upstate New York, named "Tahawus" in Mohawk "Cloudsplitter" or in Algonquin, "it pierces". It's on her Bucket List to add it to her Peak Bagged Log before she gets too rickety.

Seren Fargo, Bellingham, WA, USA

Seren began writing Japanese-form poetry in 2009. Shortly thereafter, she founded the Bellingham Haiku Group. Her work has won awards and has been widely published in several countries. A former wildlife biologist, Seren particularly enjoys incorporating her past and present experiences from the natural world into her poetry. She begins her day by feeding the birds, squirrels, and a cottontail named Muffin, many of which take food from her hands.

Ignatius Fay, Sudbury, ON, Canada

Ignatius is an invertebrate paleontologist, retired due to disability. He has been writing Japanese short-form poetry for more than twenty-five years. He is an avid reader of paleontological works and hard science fiction. In his twenties, he owned and operated three pizzerias in Sudbury. Despite frail health all his life, he intends to outlive everyone he knows. Ignatius was once approached by a neighboring octogenarian for medical advice because the neighbor had heard that Ignatius was a doctor who studied old bones.

Angela Terry, Sequim, WA, USA — Guest Editor

Angela is an award winning Pacific Northwest poet whose work has been published in numerous print and online journals and anthologies, and has been translated into several languages. Well into her seventies, Angela finally admits she'll never learn to color inside the lines.

Poets' Bios

Cynthia Anderson, Yucca Valley, CA, USA

Cynthia lives in the Mojave Desert near Joshua Tree National Park. A lifelong poet, she took up short forms just before the pandemic began and has immersed herself in them. She spent her career as an editor and project manager. Along with poetry, her passions in retirement include vegetable gardening and playing Native American-style flutes.

Marilyn Ashbaugh, Edwardsburg, MI, USA

Marilyn is a poet, nature photographer and organic gardener. She is widely published in journals and anthologies featuring Japanese short-form poetry. Hummingbird is her spirit animal.

Hifsa Ashraf, Rawalpindi, Pakistan

Hifsa is a pioneer in her country for writing modern Japanese-style micropoetry in English. Her work has been widely published. As an editor she jointly curates the Haiku Commentary blog. She is the author of five micropoetry books where she received special mention for her poetry collection, *Her Fading Henna Tattoo*, in the Touchstone Distinguished Books Award 2020 and in the Haiku Society of America Merit Book Award 2021.

Mary Jo Balistreri, Waukesha, WI, USA

Mary Jo was a concert pianist for most of her life. In 1976, she switched to harpsichord and performed up and down the East coast. She lost her hearing in 2009. Now she spends as much time writing poetry as she once did practicing. She enjoys hiking, working in the garden and gin rummy. Reading is also an addiction. She lives in with her childhood sweetheart.

Dyana Basist, Santa Cruz, CA, USA

Dyana lives on Rodeo Gulch, a riparian corridor that inspires many of her published lyric poems, haibun and haiku. Dyana's new book, *Coyote Wind*, is the story of her rollicking long-term love affair with Coyote the Mythic, and the not-so mythic. It is available through the author at openmesa@sbcglobal.net. Recently Dyana has turned her affections to a Northern Flicker wintering in an old telephone pole, she bows to it at dawn.

Sidney Bending, Victoria, BC, Canada

Sidney is a retired graphic artist living on the west coast of Canada. Her photography and illustrations have graced the inside and covers of several literary journals. Her poetry and flash fiction have been published in North America and abroad. She has a chapbook of short poems called *Mute Crows.* Together with Margaret Rutley, Sidney has published a book of haiku and related poems, *Whether Forecast*, in 2020.

Cheryl Berrong, Fairbanks, AK, USA

Cheryl is an artist, born and raised in Alaska. She began painting as a child, and her award-winning watercolors are in exhibits across Alaska and in private collections from Alaska to Mexico. A longtime member of the American Watercolor Society (AWS), Cheryl often finds herself enjoying other creative organizations, such as the American Welding Society (AWS), sometimes by accident.

Richard Bingham, Centerville, Utah, USA

Richard, a native of Utah, is a retired marketing executive, who frequently travels to Idaho to indulge his passion for fly fishing. He devotes time each week to writing interests and enjoys organic gardening. In 2018, he and his family traveled to Peru to do a humanitarian project.

Chuck Brickley, Daly City, CA, USA

Chuck Brickley's collection of haiku, *earthshine* (in its 4th printing), won a Touchstone Distinguished Book Award (2017), and Honorable Mentions in the inaugural Marianne Bluger Book Award (2020) and the HSA Merit Book Award (2017). One of his haibun was nominated for a Pushcart Prize (2018), another for a Sonders Best Small Fiction Award (2019). Once Chuck heard one of his songs drift from the window of a passing car. www.chuckbrickley.com

Alan S. Bridges, Boston, MA, USA

Alan S. Bridges works as a Patient Services Representative at a small hospital near Boston, Massachusetts. Twice he has been voted poet-of-the-year by readers of *The Heron's Nest.* His collections include *In a Flash* (Snapshot Press, 2019), *Stirring Ashes* (Turtle Light Press, 2020) and *In the Curves* (Red Moon Press, 2020). At Bowdoin College, in his first-ever pole vault attempt, Alan cleared 10 feet and decided to call it a career—way too far to fall.

Jennifer Burd, Ann Arbor, MI, USA

Jennifer is an on-line poetry teacher, an editor, and a writer of haiku, haibun,

Susan Constable, Parksville, BC, Canada

Susan mainly writes haiku and tanka, receiving her inspiration from life on the west coast of Canada. Her work is widely published in print and online journals, as well as in numerous anthologies. She has judged several contests, co-edited a couple of haiku and tanka anthologies, and acted as an editor for several years for *A Hundred Gourds, GUSTS,* and *cattails.*

Jeanne Cook, South Bend, IN, USA

In 2006, Jeanne wanted to take another poetry class at the school for adult learning, and all that was available was a haiku class. Her teacher had read a haiku that made him cry. He had determined to learn all he could about writing haiku and pass it on to others. Jeanne has been hooked ever since. She has continued to write haiku and has branched out into tanka and rengay, finding inspiration in the haiku community, of today and of the past. On the home front, Jeanne discovers that she has been trained to toss treats when her calico rings a bell.

Billie Dee, Las Cruces, NM, USA

Billy is the former Poet Laureate of the U.S. National Library Service. She earned her doctorate from UCI. After a poetry translation lecture by Billy Collins in 1994, she began studying Japanese forms in earnest. "Haiku has become a way of life for me—recording those small epiphanies that now pepper my days." After 70 years in California, Billie now resides in rural New Mexico with her family and a betta fish named Ramon.

M. R. Defibaugh, Chesterfield, VA, USA

M.R. is a newly converted rengay enthusiast whose work is influenced by love, loss, disability, and his compassion for others and the environment. He has degrees in mathematical sciences (Illinois at Springfield) and operations management (Arkansas). When not writing, you can find him playing football and golf on his PlayStation and trying to keep up with his niece and nephew. He claims to be good at both Scrabble and poker.

Janice Doppler, Easthampton, MA, USA

Janice is a retired teacher and administrator. In 2021, she won second place in Haiku Poets of Northern California's Porad Haiku Award and published *Stardust,* a collection of haiku and haibun. Bird watching and nature journaling are major sources of inspirations for her poetry and bird carving. Janice achieved her dream of doing tai chi atop the Great Wall of China – once shaking from fear of heights diminished enough to let go of the wall.

Raymond A. French, Huntsville, AL, USA

Raymond is a retired NASA project manager, wine and cocktail drinker with a camping problem, who, through rain, sleet and snow, lets Chaka take him for a walk 4 times a day. Cocktail is our trusted mascot and travel companion who oversees and approves of all mixology that occurs in PiM.

Terri L. French, Huntsville, AL, USA

Terri is a retired Massage Therapist, former barista, writer, editor, wine drinkin' tree hugger who occasionally practices yoga and has a penchant for frequenting thrift stores. She and her husband travel full-time in their RV (Poetry in Motion, aka PiM)) with their pittie mix, Chaka, and a stuffed parrot named, Cocktail.

Diane Funston, Marysville, CA, USA

Diane grows plants, harvesting the leaves into poetry. She transplants the roots into other art forms, but her garden is mainly a garden of words. She lives in the Sacramento Valley.

Joshua Gage, Cleveland, OH, USA

Joshua is an ornery curmudgeon from Cleveland. His newest chapbook, blips on a screen, is available on Cuttlefish Books. He is a graduate of the Low Residency MFA Program in Creative Writing at Naropa University. He has a penchant for Pendleton shirts, Ethiopian coffee, and any poem strong enough to yank the breath out of his lungs.

Garry Gay, Santa Rosa, CA, USA

Garry, a fine art photographer and creator of the poetic form Rengay, is author of five volumes of haiku and one of rengay. In 1989 he co-founded the Haiku Poets of Northern California, and in 1996, American Haiku Archives at the California State Library in Sacramento, CA. President of HPNC from 1989-90, 2001-2009 and 2014-2021, he founded the Two Autumns reading series. He is past president of the HSA, and in 1991 he founded Haiku North America.

Lisa Gerlits, Silverton, OR, USA

Lisa is an award-winning author of middle grade books. She is a muralist, art teacher, soup-lover, goatherd, weaver, rewilder, and believer in people. Once, on a volunteer project in southern Mexico, she machete-hacked through the jungle to stand beneath a hidden waterfall. She lives in Silverton, Oregon with three children, a Dutch husband, one exchange student, five chickens, and one cat.

collaborative haiku sequences, rengay, and free-verse poetry. She is a member of the Evergreen Haiku Study Group. In Jennifer's elementary-school days, when her father attended an evening PTA meeting, he left a magical note in her desk that read: *Udall glirb, and we split menkle with succotash. We all need a Jenny bun fluff to keep us womsat and persipideed.*

Nithya (Chandran), Mumbai, India

Nithya (Daughter of Ram) is a Postgraduate from Indian Institute of Management and manages Digital Marketing of an MNC. A passionate reader of English classics, she writes long poems, short stories and verses. An occasional writer of haiku, she plays 'veena' between her hectic schedule.

Ram Chandran, Tamilnadu, India

Ram is a Corporate Lawyer by profession and a freelance journalist. He has been writing English poems since his college days and has written poems and short stories in many literary magazines. A haijin since 2020, he has written more than 1200 haiku, haibun, senryu, tanka and haiga/photo haiku. Many of his work have been published in various prestigious print and online haiku journals and his Haiga Gallery is hosted by The Haiku Foundation.

Christina Chin, Malaysia

Christina is from the small island of Malaysia and has had self doubt since childhood. For the euphoria of small achievements, which fuels her creativity, she draws and writes haiku.

Jackie Chou, Pico Rivera, CA, USA

Jackie has volunteered for the summer meal program for children at Smith Park, Pico Rivera. When not writing, she enjoys watching Jeopardy and talent competitions, including a new show called *I Can See Your Voice.*

Sue Colpitts, Peterborough, ON, Canada

Sue started writing poetry after she retired from teaching. In 2011 her first haiku was published in *Frogpond.* Over the subsequent years, she has had a variety of oriental poetry published, including haibun and tanka, in journals and anthologies. Once an avid country gardener, she now lives in a city condo resplendent with tropical plants. Sue has learned to enjoy winter again by writing about snow and not having to shovel it.

Margie Gustafson, Lombard, IL, USA

Margie might be a reincarnation of Issa. Her book, "Haiku Very Much", is available on Amazon.

Lorraine Haig, Richmond, Tasmania, Australia

Lorraine lives in Tasmania and spends most of her time writing or gardening. Her haiku journey began in 2004 and her poems have been published in online and print journals worldwide. She's had two collections of longer poems published and is still working on her first haiku collection. Lorraine grows small eucalyptus trees and has about fifty species in her garden..

Tai Haynes, Lakewood, OH, USA

Tia Haynes is a homeschooling vegan poet from Lakewood, Ohio. When she's not corralling her two little ones, she serves as the editor of Prune Juice Journal. Her new endeavor is to learn the art of bread baking, whose secrets she has yet to unravel.

Anton R. Kelian, San Diego, CA, USA

From an early age, Anton loved the interplay of language and paint; with words and sumi ink he drew portraits and poetry. He retired from circuit design engineering and now focuses his energy on writing poetry. Anton's artworks have been featured, and his winning poems recited on blog radio. Traveled extensively; he's been to Japan many times and is hooked on Oriental poetry, which give birth to many of his themes.

kris moon kondo, Kanagawa, Japan

kris has lived in Japan for over 40 years. She inhabits a small home by a river in a village, where she writes, creates haiga and artworks, and walks collecting river stones to paint and give as inspiration and consolation to friends in difficult times. She is a constant companion to Poets on Site on zoom several times a week.

Deborah P Kolodji, Temple City, CA, USA

Deborah P Kolodji loves to wander the beaches and botanical gardens of Southern California. Her book, *highway of sleeping towns,* from Shabda Press won a Touchstone Distinguished Book Award from the Haiku Foundation. Together with co-author Billie Dee, she came in 1st Place in the 2020 HPNC rengay contest and 3rd Place in the 2021 HSA contest.

Kristen Lang, Sheffield, Tasmania, Australia

"The planet will never come alive for you unless your songs and stories give life to all the beings, seen and unseen, that inhabit a living Earth", Amitav Ghosh, The Nutmeg's Curse. All life, and the stones and rivers too. Kristen is a mountain walker with an aging labrador she assists through the rocks and streams of the foothills. Earth Dwellers (Giramondo, 2021) is her most recent collection.

Kat Lehmann, Guilford, CT, USA

Kat is a Touchstone award-winning haiku poet. She holds a Ph.D. in biochemistry and an unwavering awe of the grandiose within the minute. A potter and hiker, Kat lives on the edge of a fairy forest with her family. She is the Co-Editor of *Whiptail: Journal of the Single-Line Poem*, and her haibun collection is *Stumbling Toward Happiness*. Website: https://katlehmann.weebly.com/

Ryland Shengzhi Li, Arlington, VA

Ryland is a poet and environmental lawyer living in Northern Virginia. Poetry teaches Ryland how to pay attention and to see the beauty and interdependence of all things. He is a member of Towpath Haiku. In his free time, Ryland enjoys being in nature, practicing yoga, and learning new skills.

Kristen Lindquist, Camden, ME, USA

Kristen lives on the coast of Maine. Her e-chapbook of haiku is forthcoming from Snapshot Press in 2021. She is an avid birder who works as a birding guide each spring for the Acadia Birding Festival in Maine's Acadia National Park.

Jack Lyon, Magna, Utah, USA

Jack is a retired book editor who now publishes books and makes software for people who publish books. He loves good music, good food, and good times with his family, who kindly tolerate his increasing grumpiness.

Jayashree Maniyil, Melbourne, Victoria, Australia

Jayashree was born in India. Haiku happened to her almost ten years ago. She continues to indulge and enjoys a very casual and steady relationship with writing haiku and other related forms. She loves her food, and nibbles like a bird through the day.

Richard L. Matta, San Diego, CA, USA

Richard grew up in New York's Hudson Valley, attended Notre Dame, practiced forensic science, and now lives in San Diego with his golden-doodle dog. His haiku, tanka, and haibun are widely published with some of his work in *Modern Haiku, Frogpond, Akitsu Quarterly, Bottle Rockets,* and *Presence.*

Tanya McDonald, Woodinville, WA, USA

Tanya is known for her bright plumage and her love of birds. She lives near Seattle, Washington among evergreens and woodpeckers, and is the founding editor of the haiku journal, *Kingfisher.*

Wilda Morris, Bolingbrook, IL, USA

Wilda has degrees in political science and religious education but prefers to spend her days writing poetry, sending picture postcards to her seven great-grandchildren, and making cheesecake. She has served as president of the Illinois State Poetry Society and Poets & Patrons of Chicago. Wilda lives in Bolingbrook, Illinois, with her husband of more than 58 years.

Ron C. Moss, Leslie Vale, Tasmania, Australia

Ron is an artist and poet from Tasmania, a place of rugged wilderness, which inspires his art and poetry. His haiku and related genres have won many international prizes and his poetry has been widely published and translated into several languages. Ron has several published haiku collections that have won prestigious awards. He enjoys writing collaborative forms when he is not running towards fires and attending road crashes as a veteran volunteer fire-fighter.

Genie Nakano, Gardena, CA, USA

A poet and journalist, Genie practices and teaches yoga and meditation. With a Masters degree in Dance, she uses dance and poetry in spoken word events. Genie's books of poetry are available on Amazon and Wordpress, www.genienakano.com. Born Lenore Jean Nakano (her father loved Poe's "The Raven") but her Issei Japanese grandmother couldn't pronounce the r's. Jean became Jeanne, the sound of little bells her Grandma said.

Nika – Calgary, AB, Canada

Nika is the pen name of retired educator Dr. Jim Force. Jim enjoys creating haiku art cards and sending them out to family, friends and fellow haiku poets. He lives in Calgary, AB, with his wife and two cairn terriers. His haiku and haiga have been widely published. He is a member of Haiku Canada, as well as The Haiku Society of America.

Jacquie Pearce, Vancouver, BC, Canada

Jacquie is a haiku poet and children's book author. Her haiku and rengay have appeared in a variety of publications and received several awards. She is editor of Last Train Home, an anthology of train-themed haiku, tanka and rengay (forthcoming in 2021). Research for her kids' books has included fostering pet rats, attending War of 1812 reenactments and interviewing 8th generation Japanese wagashi-makers who might be descended from ninjas.

Robert Piotrowski, Mississauga, ON, Canada

Robert is a teacher and writer. His poems, comics, short fiction, and articles have appeared in numerous publications over the past 25 years. He spends his spare time thinking about words that don't rhyme, cabins in the woods, and rock 'n' roll.

j rap, Albuquerque, NM, USA

j rap is the proud owner of a 1915 Fairbanks-Vega open-back banjo, purchased at age 15 with money earned washing dishes in a Greek deli at the back of a drug store. He plays it old-timey, clawhammer style. He drives a 2005 Pontiac Vibe with one hubcap missing. j rap lives near the University of New Mexico, and enjoys watching the cranes and ospreys cavorting on the Rio Grande bosque.

Bryan Rickert, Belleville, IL, USA

Bryan has been published in a number of fine journals and anthologies. His haiku collection *Fish Kite* is available through Cyberwit Publishing. He is the editor at *The Living Senryu Anthology* and Co-editor of *Failed Haiku Senryu Journal*. After teaching art for fifteen years, Bryan made the career move to become an industrial coffee roaster.

Jackie Maugh Robinson, Las Vegas, NV, USA

What do you get when a truck driver marries a truck stop waitress and they take their little girl on their every trip along Route 66 for the first five years of her life, teaching her to read truck stop menus and Burma-Shave signs by age three? You get haiku poet, Me, Jackie Maugh Robinson. Here's one I recall: "*drove too long / driver snoozing / what happened next / is not / amusing*

Michele Root-Bernstein, East Lansing, MI, USA

Michele mostly devotes herself to haiku, haibun and other haiku arts. Her work appears in many of the usual places and on three large rocks along a haiku walk in Ohio. Currently, she is book editor for Modern Haiku and facilitator for Michigan's Evergreen Haiku Study Group. When she isn't coaxing the poetic muse, she's researching creative imagination across the arts and sciences, learning to garden, or otherwise turning her face to the sun.

Margaret Rutley, Bridgewater, NS, Canada

Margaret has lived in several places in Canada from the far west coast (Victoria) to the far east coast (outside of Halifax). Her lyric poetry and haiku have been published in literary journals and anthologies in Canada, the USA, the UK, Africa, and New Zealand. In 2020, Margaret published a book of haiku and related poems, *Whether Forecast*, with Sidney Bending. Some of the poems are written individually and some collaboratively.

Sigrid Saradunn, Bar Harbor, ME, USA

Sigrid, known by her friends as Siggi, spends most of her time writing short poems, painting and putting calendars and post-it notes around her house so she is not late for poets' meetings and writing sessions all over the world. In California, she zooms most of her virtual time with her poetry group.

Agnes Eva Savich, Austin, TX, USA

Agnes was born in Kraków, Poland, grew up in Chicago, and is now a university program coordinator in Austin, TX. When she's not hiking her way through Texas state parks, she plays oboe with a classical quintet, tries to get better at heavy metal bass, and floats in her backyard pool.

Dan and Julie Schwerin

Dan and Julie are a husband/wife team who have been writing rengay since 2014. While sharing much in common, their preference of writing utensils differs. Julie prefers a Pilot G-2 gel pen and Dan's best work flows from a #1 Ticonderoga pencil.

Laszlo Slomovits, Ann Arbor, MI, USA

Laszlo is one of the twin brothers in the folk music duo Gemini. In addition to his work in music, Laszlo writes both long-form poetry and haiku, and he's a member of the Evergreen Haiku Study Group. Laszlo has a knack for reaching into one of the many disorganized piles of papers in his house and pulling out just the one he's looking for. His guardian angel is looking for another post.

Sheila Sondik, Bellingham, WA, USA

Sheila is a printmaker who finds her inspiration in the world of nature. She began writing Japanese form poetry in 2010. Being part of the international haiku community gives her hope in these challenging times. She is also a member of the National Puzzlers' League, where her 'nom de puzzling' is Dragonfly.

Joshua St. Claire, York County, PA, USA

Joshua is a certified public accountant who works for a small company in Pennsylvania. He enjoys writing poetry on coffee breaks and after putting the kids to bed. His work has appeared in print, around the web, and on sticky notes on his computer monitor. He longs to replace his broken espresso machine.

Richard Thomas, Plymouth, Devon, UK

Richard's poetry collections *The Strangest Thankyou* and *Zygote Poems* were published by Cultured Llama in 2012 and 2015 respectively. He edited the poetry journal *Symmetry Pebbles*, co-edited *Thief*, and was the Managing Editor of *Ink*, Plymouth University's creative writing journal. His poetry and haiku have been published internationally. In 2021, he was selected as one Europe's top 100 haiku authors in the Haiku Euro Top.

John Thompson, Sonoma, CA, USA

John likes to get up close and personal with Aquatic Nature by paddleboarding around the rivers and bays of Northern California.

Kathleen Tice, Kent, WA, USA

Kathleen started writing haiku occasionally in the mid-'80s, after being forced to help with the publication of *Dragonfly*. She started writing haiku regularly from 2008 after moving to Washington State. Co-authored rengay and tanrenga with Richard mark a milestone in their relationship.

Richard Tice, Kent, WA, USA

Richard has been writing and publishing haiku since the mid-'70s. He was the editor of *Dragonfly* from 1985 to 1990, after Lorraine Harr. He has translated about three hundred Japanese haiku and written several dozen essays on the form.

Lew Watts, Chicago, IL, USA

Lew is the author of the haibun collection, *Tick-Tock*, and the poetry-themed novel, *Marcel Malone*. He likes fly fishing, rugby, and gin martinis at Gibsons Bar in Chicago.

Michael Dylan Welch, Sammamish, WA, USA

Michael cowrote the very first rengay with Garry Gay in 1992. Since then, his essays have been promoting rengay around the world. Michael's personal website is www.graceguts.com, which has an extensive rengay collection. Michael also enjoys racquetball, skiing and photography.

Kath Abela Wilson, Pasadena, CA, USA

Kath Abela has written poetry non-stop since she was five. Childhood bedtime stories were *Great Poems of the English Language*. She loves collaborating—free verse, haiku, tanka and cherita. Her husband, Rick, professor of mathematics and world flute collector and player, accompanies her at all her readings. She tells math conference attendees she attends to steal their words. At a conference in Tehran, she won a prize for attending all the lectures without falling asleep.

Amber Winter, York County, PA, USA

Amber expressed grief through poetry at a young age. She sadly moved away from it as she grew up. Years after another loss her writing burst out onto the pages once more. Now she enjoys writing poetry and fiction when she's not busy spending time with her thee active boys. Her husband encourages her to write more and is a constant inspiration in her pieces. Her boys have even picked up the writing bug!

Sharon Young, AK, USA

Sharon is a lifelong Alaskan, who now divides her time between Alaska and Hawaii. Her pottery is inspired by the beauty of both places, as well as the serenity of her garden and labyrinth. Not satisfied with just tomatoes and cucumbers, Sharon graced her greenhouse with marigolds and a chandelier.

Index of Poets

Tandem Submission Guidelines

Please read guidelines thoroughly prior to submitting.

Submission Windows
Spring issue: January 15 - February 15 (comes out in April)
Autumn issue: July 1 - 31 (comes out in October)

Guidelines

Tandem is a collaborative rengay-only print journal. Submissions must be in-hand by the end of the submission period.
Only one submission per submission period. A submission consists of up to 5 rengay per collaborative group. Individual poets may be a member of a maximum of three groups. Rengay must be previously unpublished and not under consideration elsewhere. 'Previously published' includes print and online journals, as well as public social media, such as blogs, etc.

Although longer versions of rengay exist, we are accepting only 6-verse rengay.
Rengay may have 2, 3, or 6 authors, in the following formats:
2 authors (A & B): A-3 | B-2 | A-3 | B-3 | A-2 | B-3
3 authors (A, B, & C): A-3 | B-2 | C-3 | A-2 | B-3 | C-2
6 authors (A, B, C, D, E, & F): choose either format for 2 or 3 authors.
A-3 | B-2 | C-3 | D-3 | E-2 | F-3 ***or*** A-3 | B-2 | C-3 | D-2 | E-3 | F-2

Each rengay must have a title. Indicate the author of each verse by placing initials next to each (these will be removed in final print form).

Submissions

Submissions may be made by email only. Put 'Tandem Submission' in the Subject Line to make sure it isn't accidentally overlooked. Please include rengay in the body of the email. NO attachments. Note any special formatting in your email text.
Include the full names of all the authors as they wish them to appear in the journal, as well as the location of each author (City, State/Province, Country).

Also include a short bio for each author (maximum of 75 words each). Each bio should include one fun fact about the author. We prefer bios that aren't lists of publications.

Send to Marcyn Del Clements — tandem.mclements@gmail.com

Selection

Submissions will be read and considered by the entire editorial staff. Rengay will be accepted when at least two of the editors have chosen the poem for inclusion. Selections will be made within 2 months of the end of the submission periods. Poets will be notified as to whether or not their poems will be included and receive emails including their poems and bios, to confirm spelling and formatting. Each subsequent issue will feature an "Editors' Pick": a favorite rengay from the previous issue.

If you have any questions regarding submissions, contact either Ignatius Fay (tandem.ifay@gmail.com) or Seren Fargo (tandemrengay.seren@gmail.com)

Rights

Tandem retains first publication rights for accepted work. Once published, rights revert to the author, but Tandem retains the right to reprint the work in future editions, anthologies, etc.

Compensation

Tandem is unable to provide compensation for contributed work.

Good Rengay:

- have a unifying theme that runs throughout. Superior rengay have more than one theme without the themes seeming forced; each verse responds, in some way, to the preceding verse;
- have verses that can stand alone as poems
- have a title that reflects the theme(s), but does not seem obvious;
- have 2-line verses that are not simply 3-line haiku written in two lines.

Rengay Information

For additional information on rengay formats and more writing tips, please check out these links:

Garry Gay, the creator of the rengay form — *Garry Gay on Rengay*
https://nc-haiku.org/pdf/RengayWriting.pdf

Michael Dylan Welch's website, *Graceguts*, has a page devoted to essays about rengay, including what it is, how to write it. The site offers several essays on rengay and a list of pertinent links. A wealth of information.
http://www.graceguts.com/rengay-essays

The Rengay Verse Form by J. Zimmerman is a webpage devoted to defining rengay and how to write them. http://www.baymoon.com/~ariadne/form/rengay.htm

Made in the USA
Monee, IL
20 April 2022

95075597R00056